A FIELD OF FIRST THINGS

A FIELD OF FIRST THINGS

Poems by
Greg Pape

Accents Publishing • Lexington, Kentucky • 2023

Printed in the United States of America

Accents Publishing
Editor: Katerina Stoykova
Cover Image: *Summer Ridge* by Clay Pape

Library of Congress Control Number: 2023948680
ISBN: 978-1-961127-01-2
First Edition

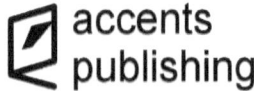

Accents Publishing is an independent press for brilliant voices. For a catalog of current and upcoming titles, please visit us on the Web at

www.accents-publishing.com

CONTENTS

Three

Four

*For Tammy, my true love & companion
for my sons, Coleman & Clay
& my brother Kevin
& for Roddy & Lulu & you*

One

ODE TO THE LETTER R

The way it starts rain and opens rose,
as long as I can remember I have loved
that sound. Though love may sound too strong

a word, I am past saving it up.
Our hurting economy needs it now,
just as the river needs its water

to meander and run, to riffle and swirl,
to roil and pool and fall on its way
to rendezvous with the sea.

In the rivers and seas of language
it is just a small boat with a small sail,
but it seems to have traveled everywhere,

rising above the waves and rolling
on the tongues from Spain to India to Tierra del Fuego.
It lives in the Arctic and the Antarctic.

It forages with the bear and prowls with the tiger.
Virgil and Homer, because it lived in them,
gave it a lasting place in the breath of their stories.

Borne on the African diaspora
it rode the tide of rhythm and blues
to the shores of rock and roll. Reborn

over and over in reading and writing,
it has a place in right and wrong.
It is first and last in remember. And

when removed from dearth, what's left?
As long as there is breath in the breather
I know its worth and am its lover.

SALT

I sat on a barstool shoulder-high to the bar
and out of the corner of my eye
watched a man tip a saltshaker over his beer.
A clandestine witness to a small wonder,

thrilled by the immediate alchemy of salt
crystals giving off a chain of bubbles
as they fell through golden light,
I felt that I had learned something.

I had heard the phrase *salt of the earth*
and imagined the sting like *salt in a wound,*
but this was something new. I was
certainly closer to a *sprout* than *an old salt.*

My stepfather called me *pumpkin,*
but I couldn't see it. I sat up straight,
squared my shoulders, sighed a little
like late afternoon, and tipped some salt

into my Pepsi, sensing that something
like creation, seen or unseen, must be,
even now, here at Andy's Bar, as we
waited for the mail boat to appear

out of the glittering distance from Punta Gorda,
a condition of the present essential as salt.

WHEN THE WORLD BEGAN TO END

It came first as a fog in the dusk
then as a scent, vaguely sweet, tinged
with burnt coal and smoldering tires
that set off an inner alarm in the lungs,
the bronchial cilia springing to attention
like a phalanx of soldiers under siege.

Then the light faded from the subtropical
night, and the whisper of the Gulf
breeze that scuffed the palmetto leaves
and pulsed with calm like moth wings
on the screen door burst into a dark roar.

We all lived in the shadow of Hiroshima.
We were all hound dogs. The Cold War
was heating up. Cuba had rolled a big
cigar and was lighting it with a flame-thrower
from a tank, and this was the night the world
was ending, I was suddenly sure.

I was ten, home alone. Jets were circling,
dropping mustard gas canisters in the yard.
I tried to squeeze under the sofa, but I
wouldn't fit. I lay on the floor with my hands
over my head surrendering to my fate,
wheezing in fear.

Then I thought about my stepfather, Stan
and his stories of Korea. The picture
hidden in his dresser drawer of a man's
blown-off leg in a boot. Adrenaline
kicked at my heart—get up and live
a little longer, fight or run.

Wasn't running how we got here
in the first place? Up until now
things seemed to be working out. We'd survived
a hurricane and a five-car pileup
on the Tamiami Trail. Stan wasn't in jail.
No one had followed us out of California.

When the hailstones tore through the top
of our Buick convertible in Kansas
Stan pulled off the highway, and we ran,
pillows and coats over our heads,
to the shelter of a farmhouse. It was dark
then, and it's dark now.

Wind took the roof off the barn, and hail
shattered the plate-glass window in the room
where we huddled with the old woman
who had opened the door for us, worried
about her husband still out in the fields.

No one died. It wasn't the end of the world,
though it seemed like it then. And now?
This is what it feels like to be alive—
alone, abandoned by the Fates, if there are
any Fates, under siege by something incomprehensible,
praying to God who is no one and everyone
to give us a break. Time to breathe in
and breathe on. Time to get up off the floor.

REPORT TO ONE WHO THOUGHT THE WORLD WAS ENDING

Listen. That cloud you thought was mustard gas,
the roar you thought from tanks and bombers tearing
open the calm night to deliver the atoms of doom,
was only the new mosquito abatement truck
blowing malathion with a small aircraft engine.

The Gulf breeze blew it off somewhere,
and you could breathe again. Even the mosquitoes
returned. Kids all over the South would hear
those trucks coming and chase after them
the way they did the Good Humor Ice Cream man.

Many of them are elsewhere. Many of them
are still living their lives. The white schoolhouse
where Mrs. Burgess stoked the coal stove between
lessons in Civics and readings from Grimm's,
for grades one through six, is a gift shop now

that sells postcards, knickknacks, lacquered shells.
You didn't die that night, but you were gone
the way you came before they raised the rent
and built the causeway, gone swaying with the waves
on the ferry headed for the mainland.

But just as the ghost of Jean Lafitte still haunts
Captiva Island, I see you sometimes sitting out
at the end of the dock gazing at the water
whispering to the fish. In a breath I join you
there, and we drift again in a continuum

of urgings and lulls, eddies of air and water,
that old muscle music of blood beating on the inner ear.

THE DOCK

Shaped like a tall T, it went out sixty feet
into the sound over the water that was always changing
from white-capping waves to a flat gray mirror
in which a pelican on a piling could stare
down its long bill and back up another.

It was a walkway over the water with no railing
that ended in a ten-by-fifteen-foot platform
with a bench on either side where one could sit
and fish, or gaze across the water until the gazer
became the water, a glittering expanse or a flat

gray misted distance that resolved into low green
clouds of mangroves, or was interrupted
by a diesel launch cutting a wake toward Blind Pass.
That was Belton Johnson motoring off
with his cast net in search of mullet, while Miriam,

our Sunday school teacher, prayed for his safe return.
I think she prayed for everyone on the island,
for Ben and Lyle Mortensen whose father
was known to beat them with a plastic belt.
Even for old Elijah, white bearded and toothless,

who frightened the children waiting for the mail boat
with stories of Saturday night lynchings
on the mainland. I know she prayed for me
and all the children she invited to her house
for Bible stories and songs on Sundays

and Disney's Mouseketeers on Wednesdays.
The Johnsons had for a while the only television
on Captiva Island. But the dock was the real church,
and the water, when it was still and gray, swarmed
with a secret life just beneath the surface

so that leaning over the wavering image
of your own face, a redfish or a manatee might
drift up out of the clouded depths and change the channel.

ON FIRST READING MOBY DICK

Let the most absent-minded of men be plunged
in his deepest reveries—stand that man on his legs,
set the feet a-going, and he will infallibly lead you
to water, if water there be in all that region.

I remember in college reading *Moby Dick*
holed up with two friends, Terry Holmes
and Waymon Kisler, in a cheap rental house
stocked with plenty of coffee and not much else.
There were tests coming up and papers to write
and page after page of surrender to the text,
leaves rustling in a grove of almond trees
planted long ago in careful rows to catch the dawns
and track the sun to dusk and filter the shimmer
of stars. How to do what needed to be done?
We'd take it head-on, that was the plan.
We'd read for an hour or two, take notes as smoke
and steam rose like ether beneath the ceiling,
then one of us would call a break and we'd sit
or pace around the table and compare notes,
read passages aloud and translate them
into our own tongues. We'd read hundreds
of books, but nothing like this.

The country was at war with itself and others.
Just as the world seemed to be quivering
and twitching like a beached whale blanketed
with flies and the doomsayers seemed saner
by the day, we had to decide what we could do
to stand up for Bob Mezey, fired for admitting
he smoked marijuana every chance he got.
We tried street theater: "I told you Aggies
to scrape the shit off your boots before
you come to class." Freedom of speech
included all the words. Our friend Joe,
laid back good looking soft spoken Joe,

once a champion high school wrestler
was just back from Viet Nam. We helped him
change the dressings on his wounded leg
four times a day so osteomyelitis didn't eat
away any more of his bone. His leg would
never be the same, but he wanted to keep
what was left. And red-headed Ron with the constant
grin and freckles like subtlest camouflage would soon
be a name cut into the black wall in Washington.
How could we stop the war? How could we make
the dream overcome the nightmare? We could march
or sit down in the street and try not to flinch
when a phalanx of cops on motorcycles came rumbling
at us as the buses arrived to haul off the arrested.
We could read on until maybe *the great flood-gates
of the wonder-world swung open.*

It took four mostly sleepless days and nights
as the house listed and the whale rolled and thrashed
in its current of words. After a while it was all
metaphor, then more than metaphor, then visions
that illuminated the walls and went dark again.
One dawn my eyes were swimming with print
I couldn't keep on the page. I tilted my head back
at the window, closed my eyes to a glowing red
ball of blubber, and smiled, knowing I was deep
inside the whale. It was almost peaceful there.
I must have dozed awhile, and when I opened
my eyes and looked back down at the book
the page was blue and the words were suspended
above the page like silvery fish idling among stars
in water. I was hooked, harpooned, nothing
left to do but go on swimming with the *ungraspable
phantom*, reading, and writing.

MIGRATION

From her fourth-floor balcony in the high-rise
beehive complex of neat or shabby low-rent
apartments known as Baptist Gardens, her last
home, she could gaze out over the parking lot
and the Mexican Market that sold fresh jicama,
tomatillos and mangos, and beyond that just
the tops of the great cranes that loaded and unloaded
ships in the port of Los Angeles. What a dance
of elephants it must have been escaped from
the circus of revival tents and coal camps
braided on the hills around Hazard, Kentucky
that led her on her life's erratic migration,
first to Cincinnati where her father, who had been
a coal miner, found work in a machine shop
running lathes, stamping and cutting steel,
grinding and shaping the earth's hard metals
into tools. There she attended Withrow High School
in the same class as my father, whom she didn't
meet until years later after her first marriage
to Fritz Venn had gone all wrong. The Queen
City of the West had its own Coney Island
and its own riverboat where gangly teens
& Miss Irene learned to dance the Charleston
on gas-lit decks adrift on the glittering Ohio.
Dancing on a moving river at night under stars
to the rhythm of a big band might well produce
a lasting bloom in memory's bouquet. Whereas
sleeping with a man so jealous he kept a snub-nosed
.32 under his pillow would be hard but good
to forget.

Remembering and forgetting, shuffling and discarding,
highlighting and deleting, mixing and matching
metaphors is all part of the art of the stories

we tell or conceal. It's a big country to run away
into, and it's a good thing there are wheels.
They must have headed west, the ex-Mrs. Venn
and the man who became my father, on old U.S. 50
driving night and day all the way to San Francisco Bay,
and then south to Los Angeles, where the whole
Kentucky clan eventually settled before some went
even farther west to the land of Aloha. Here's
a snapshot of Irene and Larry hand in hand
on the beach, smiling broadly, wearing those
frumpish bathing suits of the forties. Not long
now before the frontogenesis of mild Pacific
sunsets and the rising sun of the east produced
a mushroom cloud.

BLOOD & PERFECTION

We had just moved from a tar-papered shed
lit at night by candles and kerosene lamps,
with pastel pink and pale green bed sheets
tacked up for curtains, a tar bucket for a toilet,
to the new house Stan had built at the end
of Avenue B. What did it stand for,
I wondered, better, boy, blood? The house
had a flat roof covered with glittering white rocks,
louvered windows, and a big fireplace
of adobe blocks Stan had made of mud
and straw poured into forms one by one
and set out to dry in the sun. My mother
sang *My Blue Heaven* as she worked
in the new kitchen. She taught me to write
my name in near-perfect cursive and
showed me how to turn a small frozen
orange juice can into a bank, that when full
held exactly fifty pennies. I was learning
about work and worth, what worked
and what didn't. Having filled one small can
with pennies, I needed another. Miracles
and catastrophes abound, and in childhood
they take on an especially personal tone.
When, for instance, I set the small can
with its frozen contents out in the sun
to thaw, I lost track of time. I failed
to calculate the chemical volatility
of the hydrogen content in the concentrated
juice of the orange. I had other projects
to attend to, other explorations on which
to embark. The new bathroom waited
with its gleam of stainless steel and
immaculate white porcelain. There was so
much to consider, so much to learn.

At that time I didn't know, and certainly
couldn't spell, most of these words.
But there was something old in me
like a voice in the dark that exclaimed
and commanded in many tongues, Hebrew
maybe, Latin, English, Spanish, Chinese,
Bantu, Choctaw. And if I moved through
the moments in a reverie of concentration,
I heard words and phrases, *Behold, carpe diem,*
mea culpa, though the meaning was unclear.

But the razor blades were right there,
behind the mirror, in the new medicine cabinet,
next to the pill bottles, the toenail clippers,
and that strange instrument my mother sometimes
used to curl her eyelashes. There comes
an instant when the idea clarifies, like a black
and white photograph in its chemical bath
resolving from whiteness through the grayscale
into a focused picture. I held the cardboard
cylinder of the emptied toilet paper roll
in my left hand, and the razor blade, carefully,
between thumb and forefinger in my right,
and I could see in the transforming fire
of imagination that one straight slice
could turn a cylinder into a perfect rectangle.
What I couldn't see was that perfection
was an idea rarely if ever accomplished.
Just as I began to pull the razor down
in a straight line there was a startling *thwump!*
the bathroom window was spattered with orange
and the razor sliced through the cardboard
down through the fat meat in the heel
of my palm and stopped at the bone.

Gorgeous, the old unlikely word for altered,
comes to mind now as the crimson clouds
swirl and drain again in the porcelain sink,
and the thin scar I'll carry in my left hand
as long as I have a body is nothing but true.

MARIPOSAS

When I saw the documentary on TV of the miraculous
        migration of the monarch butterflies
I remembered waking with a fever in a room
        full of butterflies,
orange and black patterned butterflies oddly translucent
        covering the four walls,
the ceiling, the bedcovers and hovering wherever I looked.
        My own body
was cloaked with them, like a tree in the Mexican highlands.
        Mariposas they are called there.

I must have been crying when my grandmother came in,
        and when I told her
there were so many she shooed them away. Still they
        landed in her hair
and on her shoulders and followed us out into the bright
        kitchen. *Mercy mercy*
she shook her head and whistled through her teeth
        as she concocted
a potion of bourbon, honey and lemon warmed in a pan
        over stove flames.
It burned my throat as I swallowed. She held a cold rag
        to my forehead
and shooed the butterflies toward the window. *Mercy mercy*
        she sang and waved them away with her hand.

A FIELD OF FIRST THINGS

All through the days of arts and sciences, nails and glue,
  belt sanders and push brooms,
sweat clothes and knuckle-dented lockers issuing into
  afternoons of laps in the pool, or fights
in the parking lot, I felt the haunting of an old betrayal.
  I didn't even know the word for it
when that first heaven of contentment collapsed.
  García Márquez once said
that he learned everything necessary for the writing
  of *One Hundred Years of Solitude*
by the time he was eight years old. Memory is not always
  trustworthy. It lights fires sometimes
with flares of hyperbole. It winnows a week of dull hurt
  into a moment of pure pain.
In any human or animal language it's hard to say goodbye.

Sometimes a boy is closer to a dog than a man.
  And a dog can stand for a sage
of humility, or an incarnation of loyalty. Though his namesake
  was no such sage, Roderick Dhu
was such a dog. I see him, kingly collie, black, white, and tan,
  curled on the floor
of the one-chair office at Stan's Sand & Gravel, where I took
  phone messages
after school while Stan loaded rock into the crusher.
  The noise was deafening
when the river stones were broken down into gravel
  by the steel bars and teeth of the crusher.
The whole building shook. Roddy lay his head on the floor
  between his paws, turned his ears away
from the breakage of rock he must have perceived as pain,
  toward the chaparral near the river
where he knew we would go when our shift was done.

Constant companion, bodyguard, he would follow me,
        even if he were in the lead
looking back, follow me into any willow hell, briar thicket,
        cave, tunnel, or conduit pipe beneath a road.
He would stand at my hip in the schoolyard or street
        and ward off big Eugene.
If he wasn't restrained or asked to wait, Roddy would take
        a place beside me in the classroom, car, dentist's chair,
or grocery isle. Our house then was *La Casa Contenta*,
        an unlit neon sign on the valley road,
a gravel drive lined with big ponderosa pines, a yard
        of grass and cherry trees fenced by roses.
We were caretakers for the owners who had closed
        their restaurant and gone abroad.

In the coatroom near the entrance across from the cigarette
        machine I had a bed with a view
of sky through pines. Roddy slept beside me on the floor.
        Somehow together we stood for something more than
ourselves. I know they must have thought they had no choice.
        The great dragline Stan plunged into the river
for sand, and stones to crush into gravel, would be repossessed,
        and the sheriff was coming in the morning
with a subpoena. I knew nothing of that. I knew only I loved
        the place and Roddy.
How could such strong bonds be cut and turned into a story
        like a bad dream
composed in a kind of sleep, inscribed in a vanishing hand?
        Pulled out of bed in the dark
before dawn, loaded like luggage in the back of the Buick,
        I saw through the window
Roddy tied to the doorknob, a note pinned to his collar.
        He sat on the stoop, as he had been told,
good dog, his ears erect, his eyes fixed on us as we drove away.

I still see his eager, puzzled eyes, his dog smile, smell his dog
      breath back when we sat together
beside a small fire in light rain where the stored-up sun in sage,
      dirt, and bright green winter rye
was an aura of home that held us in thrall as the current
      of the Carmel River
called the sleek steelhead up from the sea.

SWEET VERMOUTH

The room off the kitchen smelled like the kitchen,
     hamburger and fried onions,
a smell she tried to wash off before she put on her makeup.
     She sipped a snifter of what she called
courage as she carefully applied the eyeliner, a smudge
     of rouge on her cheeks,
and rolled in her glossy lips to even out the red.
     Little brother was already in bed
asleep, and I had a book to read after she left for work
     as night hostess at the Elk's Club.

A full moon drifted up over the San Gabriel Mountains
     to light the whole South Bay,
the crescent beaches, the piers, the jetties, and streets
     named for jewels.
Even the alley off Sapphire Street where I had nailed
     a backboard and wire hoop
on the roof of the tool shed. I turned out the lights
     in the kitchen
to let the moonlight in and took down from above the sink
     a bottle and read the label, *Sweet
Vermouth*. I tipped the bottle to my lips to taste the name.
     It was a poke instead of a kiss,
but I was not easily dissuaded.

I knew that deeper in the bottle there must be a genie
     of jokes and laughter,
a secret mixture to lighten the mood. Courage, she said,
     and I wanted to taste it.
I squinted at the label and saw the word *wormwood*.
     Maybe that's what she meant.
One must be bold, burrow through the bitter wood to arrive
     at the light.

I walked out to the alley and turned the bottle up at the moon
      again and again
until the genie was in me laughing, and I was the bottle
      tipping over
in the oniony moonlight spilling worms of courage
      and sweet vermouth.

THE WRECK OF THE DOMINATOR

In the days of penny candy and the Penny Arcade
        where there was a metal booth
one could enter for a quarter and peer through
        a stereoscope at mostly naked women,
we children roamed the streets named for jewels,
        precious stones and women.

Most of our mothers worked at J.C. Penney's, Sears,
        Bank of America, Woolworth's, Tony's
on the pier, or the Douglas aircraft plant. Rosie
        the Riveter, with her sleeves rolled up,
her wrench, broad smile and bandana holding her
        curled hair back off her forehead

looked just like Aunt Millie, who could have posed
        for the artist commissioned by Uncle Sam
to put a bright spin on wartime factory work.
        That war was fading or mutating
into the next, and for a while it seemed
        everyone was working, leaving

us kids free to roam the streets, alleys, beaches,
        vacant lots and abandoned buildings
where we made our own territorial claims, intrigues
        and transgressions that led us
through the mists of innocence into the stark flash,
        boom and after-drift of our own small wars.

On clear days when the smog burned off
        we could see to the east the etched line
of the San Gabriel Mountains, contours rising
        and falling, a sleeping giant pillowed against sky.
To the south the oil refinery with its flaming stacks,
        like candles on the layered cake of industry.

At the edge of our town, to the west, which marked
        the edge of the continent
we looked out to the place the waves came from,
        and once, in a storm,
the Greek freighter *Dominator* rammed against the rocks
        of the Palos Verdes Peninsula.

For years it was part of the horizon, a rusting hulk
        looking back at us the way Moby Dick
eyed Ahab. Boys, it seemed to say, these ventures
        on the vast Pacific end in shipwreck, whether their genesis
is the foghorns of boredom, revenge, or bright bells
        and bon voyage.

THE WAVE

We got up in the dark in our separate rooms,
closed the doors quietly and walked out barefoot
listening for the sound of surf. We gathered in pairs
or groups of three or four with our boards and stood

watching as the dawn rose over the city at our backs,
watching the swells, the lines of waves coming in
in the first dim light, sizing up the break at Avenue C,
Topaz, and Sapphire Streets from the top of the sand cliffs

along the Esplanade. We smoked or spoke
in low tones in a reverie of gazing as the waves
formed out of the incoming swells, watching them peak
and feather as they broke in lines to the right

and left then collapse into the rumbling froth
we called *soup* that hissed and sizzled into the sand.
The left break off the jetty at Sapphire Street
had the best shape, so we walked our boards down

the stairs, past the ice plant covered with a fine
salt rime. We waxed our boards with squares of paraffin
or roughed up the poured-on wax jobs with handfuls of sand,
then paddled out through the soup and the swells

to sit and gaze *outside*, looking along the horizon
for the wave with the most promise, and choosing one,
adjusting position by paddling out or left or right
so that we might stroke at just the right time

to align our bodies and boards as one
with the momentum of the wave, so that we might
enter the wave and be borne along in its brief life.

DICK DALE & THE DEL-TONES

Do you remember Dick Dale & The Del-Tones?
Probably not. You could google them.
They played at the Rendezvous Ballroom
lost Saturday nights on Balboa Island.
A left-handed lead guitar, a drummer
who loved to crash the cymbals, a rhythm guitar
and bass who made the floorboards bounce.
Let's Go Trippin' was the surfer's anthem
years before *Good Vibrations* and the Summer
of Love. We'd drive down Pacific Coast Highway
and slip in among the crowds and dance
until 2 am when they'd flash the lights
and we'd have to leave. Exhausted
we'd fall asleep in the back seat of someone's car
in the parking lot, and wake at dawn to the sound
of surf, pounding surf if we were lucky,
shoulder- or head-high waves we'd ride for hours
as if that was our very reason for being,
as if that was what we were born for.

THE HORSESHOE PIER

It was a city unto itself
built above the waves of the South Bay.
Its great pilings sunk in the sand,
anchored in cement, were once the trunks
of trees that grew for over a century
in the Sierras. On days when the sea
was rough, when swells were strong
you could feel them sway as they
must have swayed in the mountain winds.
I can feel it now as I stand here
conjuring in the cold, looking out
at the dark lines of swells coming in
from the Pacific, or down a braided line
that disappears into the water where
the baited hooks wait to be taken.
Sardines shimmer in galvanized buckets,
or tug lightly at the weighted lines.
A loose society forms and dissolves
above the waves. Men and women, old
and young, leaning on the rails, gazing
out to sea, or looking down into water
where perch nudge barnacles or a jelly fish
drifts with the current, a small transparent
parachute with frayed lines suspending
nothing. So what do *these* lines suspend?
A place of living peace, a meeting place
where one could catch a dogfish
or a Spanish mackerel, or hear for the first
and only time a phrase in Estonian—
a girl's uncle, entertaining her as knight errant,
got his head stuck in a bait bucket: *unholy*
this darkness of the Czar's faulty armor, free
this fool from the scales on his eyes, call
the fire department! Is that what he said,

trying to dislodge the bucket from his head?
Or one could marvel at the opalescent gleam
of pooled rainbows from the deep
lining an abalone shell, or read the red sign
on the window of the Pizza Shack, *Peligro!*
Queso Caliente! That rich fish-scented,
tar-stained languor that drew the truants
and the unemployed, the budding graffiti artists
of the pornographic displays in the public toilets,
the fishers and feeders of gulls, the tourists
with their sacks full of seashells and T-shirts,
the young girls who left finger and lip prints
on the green tanks where lobsters scrambled
over lobsters in glass corners, drew me then
and draws me now. Maybe the grand message
of its peculiar architecture was not just
open for business twenty-four hours, but *come aboard
one and all, and good luck.*

ON THE JOB

A brilliant sheen of water
from the yellow tanker
beats down the dust.
The desert seems to drift a little
under the heat waves.
The man driving the tanker
wants to close his eyes. Three miles
an hour, the engine droning, dust
and heat coming up through the floorboards
and in the window, springs in the seat
rocking. He blinks. He lets his heavy lids
rest a moment closed—a red velvet curtain
is drawn, afterimage fades, surf washes
smoothly up the sands, foam hisses
as it recedes and the world begins
to tilt and slide as the truck leaves
the road and jolts over a rock.

This has happened before.
He opens his eyes, turns the big
steering wheel gradually to the left
and eases back onto the road,
then pushes his knee against the wheel
and unclasps his belt, runs the belt
between the handle of the door,
and cinches it tight to hold the wheel
on the straight line the road runs
out into the desert for miles
until it disappears in a mirage
of miniature blades and dozers floating
above the land.

        And the land out there
is as insubstantial as money, a hundred dollar

bill, say, he found once when he was a kid
and held a small magnifying glass over,
concentrating the rays of the sun
until a spot darkened and smoked
and an ashen ring spread out
around a hole he could hold up
and look through at anything he wanted.

PEACHES

Those mornings, rising from sleep before dawn
in Fresno to drive down Highway 99
in that old yellow pickup, my Palomino,
to work in the peach orchards outside Kingsburg,
were briefly cool and glorious as the sun began to rise
and I sang lines and phrases of songs
burning through the static on AM radio—
ride, Sally, ride ... and *the wind cried Mary* ...
I love you Suzy Q ... and *Go ask Alice* dissolved
into *I can't get no Satisfaction* ...
The morning was a woman who might have loved me,
if I didn't have to go to work.
Even the dark-eyed beauty with the sunny cleavage
and basket of grapes on the Sun-Maid Raisin sign
outside the packing houses at Selma
seemed to look longingly right into my eyes.

But when I pulled into the dirt road beside the ditch
and parked my truck next to the other trucks
all the men smoked and stared at their boots
as Ruben, the foreman, explained the workings
of the new mechanical peach harvester and his plan
for the day. We would grip the limbs
with hydraulic arms, throw a switch, and shake
those sweet peaches out of their trees.

By nine the sun was hot and the air was thick
with dust and peach fuzz. The hydraulic shakers
made the peaches fall like softballs on the padded bleachers
that fit around the base of each tree, then the peaches
rolled onto a conveyor that dumped them into a bin.
Sometimes the shakers broke a limb or snapped off
a branch that whacked one of us in the head. We tied
our straw hats on with twine and wore bandanas

over our faces like train robbers. When, mercifully,
the machine broke down, we knew why.
It rattled its own bolts loose, just as it rattled
our teeth and jarred our bones.
We would lie down on the ground exhausted,
hoping Ruben would have to go to town for parts.
And there in the sudden quiet of the orchard,
looking up through the leaves and voluptuous
slightly swaying peaches touched by glints
and filtering rays of sun, I heard the voice of T'ao Ch'ien—
how I long to rise in thin air
and ride the wind in search of my own kind.

Then the engine started up again
and drowned out the voice of T'ao Ch'ien.
Then I heard the voice of Ruben.

PARTY TIME

There was a time when the days
could go anywhere, bouncing like beads
of mercury freed from the confines of a cylinder
used to measure an aspect of the weather.

After the glass broke, and the party was over,
someone had to clean up, gather the shards,
run the vacuum, dampen a page from the newspaper,
wipe the floor. Many days, those bright toxic

metallic spheres, those small sparkling fragments
that could cut through flesh, got lost
of their own volition. Others seemed to bloom
suddenly out of the soil of ennui, or take off

like a sentence in search of a new verb.
And then the party was on again.
Someone I recognized as myself
was down there in the crowd at Playland

shuffling and bouncing to the beat
of The Grateful Dead. A woman dressed
in a flag introduced herself as Turtle
and offered me a brownie. The music

lifted me through iridescent fog, flew me
like a kite, and lay me down below the banks
of speakers bookending the stage where I gazed up
at the flames and fret sparks issuing from Garcia's fingers.

Whatever I was then, reverence to reverb,
I was full to the brim and overflowing, the doors
to perception banging in the wind, someone
off in the distance waving, calling me in.

ROXY'S BAND

They were trying to make music, not money,
but music didn't work to pay the rent. Roxy did,
in a topless bar in the city, because she was a believer
in their tenuous talents. For her belief she suffered
the usual indignities. She sold her secret beauty
for their sake, and the music they would make.

They would get high. They would get down,
set up the drums, tune the guitars, adjust the reeds,
soak the harmonicas, turn up the amps, jam and riff
until their shirts were damp with sweat. One two
blow the blue train down the track and back.

And when the sun settled down beyond Mt. Tam
and they'd break for a smoke on the porch, on her
night off, she could hear the drums and bass lines
and sometimes a guitar solo coming from up the road
or from some hollow in the hills around Lagunitas,
all the bands for miles working on their sets, jamming
the stars out. Big Brother, Bloomfield, Sons of Champlin,

The Floating Opera, rocking the pine- and pot-scented
woods of Marin. Harps and hounds howling blues
through the trees and all the young rockers shining
their axes, balancing glass top hats on their heads,
counting time in accelerated heart beats
through the throbbing black mesh of their amps,

and Roxy, eyes closed, swaying to the beat,
her slight smile rocking, floating, a small boat
on the waves of sound, dancing now with all her clothes on.

LAS LOMAS

Three kinds of doves
lived outside my windows.
The stout white-winged of the desert
adorned with lavender eye shadow,
mourning doves moving in and out
of shade calling for the lost,
and the small, speckled Inca,
no more than a handful of gravel,
nervous yet bold in the company
of fiercer birds. Wild pigs,
Sonoran javelina, came also
to snuffle the birdseed between dusk
and dawn. The mother javelina
leading her three piglets
to the scraps of lettuce and potato skins
thrown out with the birdseed
made me long for children
of my own. The room where I worked
was sunk three feet below the desert
and windows spanned the western wall
of the small, low-ceilinged rock house.
I had a big green overstuffed cast-off chair
I had found on a curbside in Tucson
aimed at the windows, the sunsets
and dawns, and my lights illuminated
the nightlife of the desert
attracting lacewings, spiders, and sphinx moths,
deer mice, snakes, and great green Colorado
River toads whose poisonous skins
would be lethal to any predator
who tried to eat them. Months
I sat in the chair reading and making notes,
studying for my exams, tumbling
through waves of Whitman's and Thomas's

syntax, turning down pages of *The Plague*,
rowing against hope all night
across Lake Maggiore to watch the sunrise
light the candelabras of saguaro
outside my window. I slept odd hours
and my dreams flashed and faded
like patchwork for quilts spilling
from a trunk, not the patterns with names,
the drunkard's path, wild goose chase, log cabins,
wedding rings and stars, but the cut pieces
of odd cloth before the salvage work of hands,
all those fragments I would have to assemble
sooner or later into some sensible vision
to live by. Start with the hills, I thought,
las lomas, and the doves, white-winged,
mourning doves, and the little handfuls
of gravel called Incas, nervous yet bold
and eager to live whatever life is set before them.

STARS: FORT APACHE/THEODORE ROOSEVELT INDIAN BOARDING SCHOOL

Fires burn in old wine bottles lying in the weeds
            at the side of the road. Fallen stars.
Sundown spreading molten waves, or is it blood and bruises,
            in the Arizona clouds. Mountains
that seemed to define the far edge of the world in the morning
            are pressing in, turning me one way
and another even as they fade and sky mutes and cools
            to twilight.

Tired of driving, but it's tiredness I could push through,
            could drive until dawn if I had to,
could go on over the dark White Mountains, cross the plateau,
            burn through Painted Desert, wind
my way through the stone maze and into the salt-laden heart
            of Utah if I had to,
but I have an appointment at Fort Apache.

When I arrive after dark Mrs. Keesay shows me my room
            in the boys' dorm, once the barracks
of the cavalry whose job it was to try to tame the Apache.
            Mrs. Keesay, whose great grandfather,
Alchesay, was a legendary scout, opens the door to a room
            with seventeen beds, usually reserved,
she says, for the visiting team, but tonight and the rest of the week
            it's all mine to share with the ghosts of the frontier.

Before I fall asleep I might remember stories I read,
            how the young Apache
named Gokhlayeh, One-who-yawns, lost his mother, his wife,
            and his three young children
to a bloody ambush by Mexican soldiers. Driven mad by grief
            and desire for revenge
One-who-yawns became Geronimo. Geronimo, Chato, Loco,
            three Apache chiefs

who survived the wars were all sent off to prison in Florida.
        In old age Geronimo
tended a melon patch in Oklahoma.

Twenty-five years ago, lying in one of those seventeen
        beds, I don't know
what I was thinking when I wrote in my journal the first
        few lines of this poem,
but next morning from the dorm window at Fort Apache
        on a rise a mile or so outside
Whiteriver, Arizona I could see an airstrip with a faded
        orange windsock
and past that a mill and stackyard where the graded corpses
        of ponderosa pines steamed in the sunrise.

Each weekday morning Apache mill workers ran to the end
        of the airstrip and back.
Some raced, some jogged, some plodded along in the dust
        behind the pack dying for a smoke.
The school, too, was run on a military model. The common
        crime, AWOL, got you hours,
punishing time on a work detail. You could scour toilet bowls,
        peel potatoes, scrub blood
from linoleum in the dark basement where Saturday night
        lovers huddled and fights flared.

After classes with sons of many tribes, descendants of warriors,
        Chiricahua, Mescalero, Shoshone, Paiute,
Hualapai, boys, sixth, seventh, and eighth graders from as far
        away as Fairbanks, as close as Whiteriver,
from Warm Springs, Gallup, Supai, I played basketball
        on the hard courts in front of the dorm.

In the middle of a game of twenty-one with Darrin, Tyrone,
        and Fred, five foot four,

Mescalero Apache, whose play was fierce and driven,
        all our fine dry ego feathers
were caught off guard by a hard rain so shirts, skins, and stern
        game-faces dripped, fires cooled,
and laughter slowed the game down but made it better.

To bring some poetry into the mix was my job, to help
        with reading, writing,
and the affirmative action of imagination. We started
        with exercises from Kenneth Koch's
Wishes, Lies, & Dreams. We wrote letters home and letters
        to ourselves and moved on to origin stories.
Edi from Yakima, MVP on her fast-pitch softball team,
        also on probation
for robbery and breaking and entering, wrote:

> *The earth was created by God. Many years ago*
> *there was another world, then one of the big*
> *green stars fell from the sky. Every body*
> *ran around and screamed. The mountains now*
> *are big department stores. The bumps on the ground*
> *are people. The star covered everything except*
> *a "lady and man." They ran into each other*
> *fell in love and had babies for the world.*
>
> *Note: I think there were alot of worlds before*
> *but stars keep falling.*

Tonight, under stars wherever and whoever we are,
        I call the roll again to hear the names—

Jennifer James, Lorna Conger, Eliza Brown, Tim Escalanti,
Harlan Wilder, Roy Lewis, Raymond Valencia, Delton Soos,
Elwood Honeycot, Ralph Jackson, Weldon Jones, Ernestine Stevens,
Marsha Watahomigie, Lonnie Manakaja, Johnny Chiago,

Fred Washington, Darrin and Tyrone Tewee,
Reno Kane.

NOT LIKE A DREAM OF FREEDOM

The sun shines on everything.
        On the museum with its glass skylights
in the ceiling angled just so
        to take in only the north light.
On new grass pushing up
        through cracks in the asphalt.
On the waxed blood-red hood
        of the Cadillac in the parking lot.
On the razor wire spiraling along
        the perimeter fence of the Julia Tutwiler
State Prison for Women
        like an eerie visual music meant
to clarify and insinuate
        the human potential for pain.

And the sun shines on the white laundry
        hung out to dry in the yard
where soon the buzzer will sound
        and the inmates will be let out
to take whatever measure of freedom
        they can still dream
with their lunch of beans and white bread.

And then after lunch a few of the women
        will go to poetry session,
and when that's over Angela
        will take the poet aside,
the first man she's seen in months
        who wasn't a guard or a shrink,
and read him the poem
        she wouldn't show to the group.

He will carry the poem with him,
        not like a dream of freedom,

that was Langston's poem,
    unless shared in common
    like sunlight and like air,
    the dream will die for lack
    of substance anywhere ...
No, not like a dream of freedom,
    but like a secret hurt told,
given into a stranger's care.

Two

AUNT GODIVA

My great great (etc.) aunt Godiva
was a modest, compassionate woman,
full of kindness and respect
for her poor neighbors.
Stripping the gold foil from a chocolate
and tossing it, we may imagine
a naked lady on a naked horse.
But before we bounce and jiggle off
through the woods to the next thing,
let's consider her motivation.
Old feudal Duke So-and-So, her husband,
decided to fatten his purse
on the backs of the poor folks
who worked the land. Remind you of anyone?
Aunt Godiva pleaded with the Duke
to give them a break. Here's the deal,
the Duke, who must have been really
full of it, himself, said, Ok
you ride that big white horse of mine
nude as a toadstool, naked as a nestling
through the whole of the village
in broad day, and I will rescind the tax,
and, by God, she did it. Not a villager,
out of decency and respect for her,
parted a curtain to watch her proud ride,
except that one bastard, Tom,
also, most likely, some distant kin of mine.

RAG PICKERS, NEW YORK, 1896
(Photograph by Alice Austen)

The hand carts of the rag pickers
bow under the weight of burlap sacks
stuffed with cast-off cloth. One man
sits resting on the curb, the other
leans against his rag sacks holding
a tin bucket, looking into the future,
the question in his eyes, how much?
Behind them a wall of posters: *Lost
Strayed or Stolen*, a musical comedy
playing at the 5th Ave. Theatre, the question
of the day. These men are their own horses
at rest before lifting and hauling
the half-ton carts with sixteen-spoke
wooden wheels through the steaming clumps
of horse dung in the cobbled streets.
A half-naked woman with a bouquet
of hops in her hand straddles an eagle in the clouds
above the words *Rochester Beer*. Another
woman shakes her bare hips and beats
a bass drum hung from a strap
over her shoulders. A smiling elf
and a black goat dance to the unheard
beat below something unseen "light as a feather"
falling on the sidewalk near the boy
in knickerbockers gazing across the street.
Top-hatted, stripe-trousered Uncle Sam
taps his big-booted foot and holds up like a trophy
a bottle of *Pabst Malt Extract*—
The Best Tonic It gives Vim and Bounce—It Braces.
The rag pickers, their backs to the chatter
of the billboards, rest a moment under the words
then rouse their inner horses, lift the hames,

and begin slowly again pulling the big-wheeled carts
through the streets of New York.

WAKING TO RAIN

Waking to the sound of rain on the metal roof,
a soft pattering. Rain, I think, melting the snow
turning the roads to slush and ice.
Then I hear a louder tapping and look up
to see birds on the skylights pecking
at the beaded raindrops, a dozen or more
Bohemian waxwings fluttering, slipping
on the domed plexiglass or standing balanced
on small, clawed feet, drinking rain,
peering down at me where I lie, marveling
at this odd new place they've found, like clear ice
over a deep pool. I see cockades of cinnamon
feathers above the black eye-stripes, the brushes
of the tails as though dipped in yellow paint,
the white streaks and red spots on the wings,
and the dark eyes that look down at me.
A wave of joy runs through my body.
I close my eyes, open them, and the birds
are gone. The skylights are empty gray
rectangles, and one of them leaks into a
bucket I've placed beside the bed. Lucky
day, I think, auspicious morning like no other.
Then I remember the lavender balloons
tied to the street signs, marking the way
to the Alvarez home up the road, their
beautiful daughter, Kirsten, killed last week
when her car slid on the ice, how it must be
there this morning waking to rain, rain
that falls on the daughterless room
Mr. Alvarez passes, sliding on ice, turning
the wheel to no avail, on his way to the kitchen.

JAKE

In memory of Jacob Brookins

We drove to the Mogollon Rim
in his old sun-faded red pickup truck
bouncing on springs over rutted two-track
roads, through corridors of slanting light
and shade of massive ponderosa pines,
open elk parks, to the rocky edge
of the canyon where we'd make our descent
to find the sweet nearly secret sanctuary
of Clear Creek where Jake had taken
his and others' kids and friends over the years
to share the hidden wonders and waters
of the Arizona mountains. We had passed
a couple of log trucks laden with the dismembered
corpses of giant ponderosa pines, and realized
that we were witness to a theft, an ongoing
theft from the past, present, and future
of this once wild place, where now
even the sound of the wind in the pines
was marked, graphed, and slated for bid.

What lingering sadness or disgust we felt
in the dust of those trucks hauling away
the venerable and gorgeous trees
was replaced by the focused effort of the climb
down into the canyon where wrens
and the water warbled below us.
Jake led the way, moving deer-like down
the slope, now and then looking back
over his shoulder, the descent steep, the air
in the canyon cool and woven with sounds
and scents of water, muted humming, distant
bells, brushes, and strings of water against rock.
When Jake stopped, I stopped, to listen,

breathe and focus on the next line of descent,
the next few steps into the sun-drenched heat
of the canyon where cool water called.

We came to a sandbar on the creek,
a great alcove of rock over sand, almost
a cave, a sheltered place where Jake
had camped before. Others had camped
there too, the wall blackened by many fires.
A spring seeped from the wall at the downstream
end of the alcove and a matted tangle of vines,
wild grape, spread out green along the sand
at the edge of the creek as though it were
an ornamental border planted to enhance
the space. Small trout were rising to a hatch
of light mayflies. A hummingbird buzzed in
to check out the red flower of Jake's bandana.
Jake the stonemason, the blacksmith, Jake
the painter, the potter, son, father, friend.
Jake who lived a life of artful work,
who shared his love of secret places.

CRANES

In memory of Peter Matthiessen

Heard the voice of Sandhill cranes,
scanned the sky, blue to darker blue
above the yellowing cottonwoods,
and saw six of them circling high
above Eagles Point, the whites of their underwings
flashing as they spiraled up, gaining altitude,
getting their bearings, then flying off
in formation toward the southeast.
Even after I lost sight of them
I could hear their purling voices.

Fishing once on the Bitterroot River
with Jon and Peter, we heard that voice
as we drifted along a cut bank. What is it, we wondered.
It was strange yet familiar. Wild Turkey?
Grouse? Then Peter remembered. Sandhill Crane,
he said. And we could see it clearly
as if it stood tall in its red beret
on the bow of the boat.

Now the summer is over.
The Bitterroot cranes have raised their young
in the hay meadows along the river.
Their wild long-legged dancing and mating,
nesting and grasshopper grazing done
as they fly now toward the wetlands in the south.

Peter loved the cranes, and worked to save them
as if they were siblings from the blind mechanics
despoiling their lands, poisoning their waters.
Birds of Heaven, he called them.
Now he must be one himself.
His words carve a spirit that looks back at us

crane-like and calls from clouds
or shady groves across the river.

PEOPLE WHO WERE NOT THERE

From the draw below the house
a buck, a whitetail with wide antlers
came stalking, nose to the ground.

Then two more bucks appeared.
We were talking on the phone,
late afternoon, the sky clear and blue,

the sun about to go down behind
the snow-mantled peaks of the Bitterroots.
Two bucks faced each other, stared

a moment, then clashed antlers.
The big one drove the other back
and twisted his neck and nearly flipped

the smaller buck onto his side, who
backed off and walked away. Then
I saw the doe watching from higher

on the hillside as the big buck stalked
her scent, zigzagging, nose to the ground.
You were telling me about your visit

with Mona in the hospital, any time now
you said. She was seeing people
who were not there, and snakes coiled

in the corners of the room. Oh Mona,
you said, dear dear Mona. The doe,
as the buck approached, turned her back

to him and flicked her tail as he
ran his nose up her leg and quickly
mounted her. I looked away

a moment. Poor Mona, I said,
then told you what I saw.

THE FENCE

Because the neighbors have dogs, they fenced
their five acres with goat wire, so-called
for the six-inch square grid of wire
too stout for a goat to chew. It works
for dogs, but it's hard on deer. Fawns
trying to keep up with their mothers
have been known to get snared
in a goat-wire fence and die of hunger,
or worse, dogs. Last week on my way
out the road I came on a full-grown doe
with her rear hoof snared in the top strands
of the fence. She hung upside down
thrashing in panic, whipping her contorted
body and flailing her sharp hooves
against the fence. A magpie watched
from a nearby post. The doe rolled
the big brown globe of her eye, showing
a crescent of rare white, terror at my
approach that stopped me and made me
avert my eyes. Easy there I said
trying to sound calm, trying to make
myself small as I reached for her leg
and grasped it below the hoof bleeding
at the hair line where the wire held her,
cutting into her ankle the more she
thrashed. Leaning my head away
avoiding her sharp right hoof kicking
wildly toward me I tugged at the wire,
but couldn't free her. I backed away,
squatted down and tried to quiet my
breathing. Wire-cutters, pliers, something
to bend the wire. She flailed and flipped
over bending back on her spine, trembling
like a hooked fish. I remembered

the little multi-tool I kept in my truck,
knife, screwdrivers, and a small slide-out
pliers. I spoke to her as I found them
easy there, easy girl. I grasped her leg
again and pried the wire loose and freed
her hoof. Her body dropped exhausted
to the ground, and she rolled into the fence
with a deep sigh, her legs curved through
the goat wire as though holding on, she
lay there still, her eyes closed as if her
heart had given out. She might have died
of fright. Who knows how long she'd hung
struggling, caught in the fence? Then
her ear twitched and her eyes opened
and in an instant she rolled away from
the fence and was up and running, blood
dripping from her hoof, running to join
the others who had waited and watched
from the pines.

SKETCH OF THE BUDDHA ON A SIDEWALK IN CHICAGO

Where can one go to find peace in the city?
How about the corner of Clark & Erie
in the middle of the crowded seven o'clock sidewalk,
people rushing to dinner and the night's entertainment,

Sweet Home Blue Chicago or HBO and *a big fat dube*,
horns and sirens and jostling taxis turning
the corner of time, like a steadfast boulder
in a human stream he sits zazen

holding his Buddha still
in the midst of clamor, eyelids nearly closed, palm
cradling palm, thumbs nearly touching, legs
in full lotus on the pavement,

air of the great city by the lake his breath, breath
drawn in, swirling petals in an eddy, and breath
released, flower of exhaust and starlight.
Arm in arm, a couple walks by, two heads

leaning together, four legs walking in rhythm,
amazed by the creature they are
they bow slightly as they pass.
A woman stops them with a sad story,

homeless from Memphis, cold and broke,
help me feed my children, I got no socks on my feet.
The man hands her a five, and the woman
slips off her shoes, rolls down her hose,

hands them over to the homeless mother
from Memphis. And the Buddha
smiles slightly as the human stream flows.

DANDELIONS

How can you hate them? They are like little suns,
cool yellow flames that don't hurt your eyes.
Tribes of them gather in grass, the unsprayed grass

in public places where the keepers don't care,
or the neglected yards of the working poor,
or the gardens of the celebrants of the sun.

Most are marked for death before they bloom,
death by herbicide, death by mower.
Some few still ferment them into wine, some

harvest the greens for food. Children
and those who remember the small thrills
of childhood notice the delicate white seed-globes

in the grass. They pluck the stems and blow
them into each others' faces, or blow them
into the air and watch the seeds drift down

in the distance like parachutes. The thrill
is the consequence of breath, the soft power
of dissemination, the lightness, the drift.

IN ROME

In Rome they are scrubbing the grime
from the Colosseum. In Aleppo
they are rolling barrel bombs
from helicopters onto school yards.
A man on the street in New York
is asked, "When are you frightened?"
"Each morning when I wake, old,
crippled, and no one wants my art."
Patterns of sun and shade
on the lined page. Bees just over
head, their wings pitched
like vibrating strings, move from blossom
to blossom in the apple tree
gathering nectar and spreading pollen.
Many have landed, grasping stamens
and rubbing anthers, rapt
for a moment, wings stilled as the orchestra
of moving bees plays its vibrato notes,
as an oscillating fan hums in a summer room.
Five white petals streaked with pink,
yellow clusters of anthers at their centers.
Distant clouds above the mountains
in Montana seem to rest like a bedded herd,
but they too are moving. Nothing stops,
a drifting fragrance, an ecstatic peace,
a far ribbon of black smoke rising.

Three

ROAD TRIP WITH LULU

By January in Montana, one begins to dream
of long walks in the desert, a light pack,
some dried fruit, and a canteen, or a south-bound
highway with a shimmering horizon so far off
if the car broke down there'd be no way
to walk there by nightfall, or a beach, any beach
with sand and waves and the intermittent rush
and hiss of saltwater smoothing the shore
and licking your bare feet like some immense
and friendly dog. So, when Annick asked me
to drive Lulu to Santa Barbara in Bill's car,
I saw it as a chance to bond with my new friend
on a long drive into the sun. But first

we had to make it over Monida Pass.
I had the radio, many stations wafting
on the solar wind, Rachmaninoff dissolving
to soft rock or weather reports from Pocatello.
The strongest signals declaimed *Jesus is risen*, or
my favorite color is camouflage. Lulu dozed
in the back seat like a princess on her palanquin.
What could she be thinking? *My new friend
must not know the way home,* or *we are going
someplace other than home.* Surely her nose
sensed the new terrain, the roadkill we passed,
the rich shaggy air of Herefords hovering like
a cloud around Lima, Montana. Lulu dozed
in the mystery of her senses, now and then
lifting an eyelid or an ear at some harsh note
from the radio or some burst of road-song
from the new friend. When I hollered
Wake up! Idiot at a trucker drifting his big rig
between the lines like a hula dancer, Lulu
pinned me with her gaze in the rearview

and sat up reporting for any duty the captain
called for. Long stretches the road smoothed
and lulled through vacancies of geological time
between upheavals. Pines and firs withered
and dwindled to buckbrush and sage. Then we were
skimming the vast volcanic sprawl of southern Idaho
misapprehended by the Department of Energy as wasteland
consigned to nuclear experiment. Out there
in the blackened distances of western expansion,
small enclaves of habitation; Mud Lake, Arco,
Atomic City. Lulu's paws flicked in a retriever's dream,
perhaps of partridge and chukar. I chewed
the butt end of a Slim Jim and looked for a rest area.
And found one in the Caribou National Forest
somewhere between Pocatello and the Utah State Line,
where Lulu emerged from the backseat with the joy
and giddiness of an astronaut stepping onto the moon.
Rest was not what Lulu did there. A quick glance
at the surroundings and her nose plunged earthward.
She leaned her weight into the leash and pulled me along
as she read the recent and ancient history of the place,
zigzagging through dry grass and thornbush, working
her nostrils in degrees, from quick sniffs to long
contemplative drafts. Clearly her nose turned pages
of earthy script no human has the power to decipher.

With the poise and dignity of a panther, and just as black,
she posed in the sun, then added her strophe
to the verse she scanned. Virgil to my Dante, she led me
down a steep ravine to a dry streambed, a little Styx
one could cross in a single step, to show me the bones.

Aridity is a defining condition of life and death in the West.
Bones not eaten whiten. Bones of some small being Lulu

would have crunched and swallowed fast had I not restrained her.
Bones like glyphs on the darker sand made me wonder
who had died here. It was John Gardner, I think, who said
there are only two stories in the world, a man or a woman
goes on a journey, or a stranger comes to town. It may be
that only point of view keeps us from seeing that it is
the same story. Endless variations, limited insights. After
a bowl of water and a Milk-Bone, we were on the road again.

From Tremonton, where I-84 comes together with I-15,
to Spanish Fork, a hundred miles of dodgers and huggers
jockeying for position, traffic so clotted, the arteries
so constricted with the plaque of vehicles a massive embolism
seemed ever imminent. I remembered back in the days of
carburetors two lanes of well-spaced traffic cruising at 55,
a clear view of the bright spires of the Mormon Tabernacle
from ten miles out, while the great Salt Lake gleamed
a steely blue and stretched beneath its birds into the hazy distances.

Now as the sun dipped below visors, we southbound drivers,
tending westerly through the rush, were forced by the flow of traffic
to contend with the glare, a pillar of fire falling
through our windshields. Semi-blind and in various states
of distraction and denial, we sped through the promised land.
Then a swarm of red bees, brake lights, tires shrieking,
cars swerving, and Lulu sliding against the shotgun seat
as the flow of traffic halted. The shrill wavering cry
of an ambulance drifted toward us over idling engines.

Stalled in traffic but so far unhurt, I took a deep breath.
Lulu groaned a dark dog sigh of exasperation
mixed with acceptance of purely human foolishness.
Then she turned three times on her bed
and settled back down into some approximation of sleep.

On the road ahead there was suffering and wreckage.
But we were headed to Santa Barbara. Just as the Mormons,
who built this sprawling series of habitations on the western
slopes of the Wasatch Range found sanctuary here,
we would too. Under the darkening shadow of the Angel Moroni,
we would extricate ourselves from the interstate,
glide down the off-ramp at Lehi, a place named
for the white-bearded saint who followed the Liahona
into the wilderness, and check into the Best Western,
where Lulu would check out the parking lot
and the dead grass around the motel
with the sincere intensity of a priest reading scripture.

After an hour of ESPN and The Weather Channel,
I pulled open the drawer beside the bed and found,
not the Gideon Bible, but the Book of Mormon,
and read this summary of the news of the world
in the voice of the angel: "And behold it is the hand
of the Lord which hath done it. And behold also,
the Lamanites are at war one with another;
and the whole face of the land is one continual round
of murder and bloodshed; and no one knoweth the end of the war."
Beside me on the floor, oblivious, Lulu curled in peaceful sleep.

Day two. 5 a.m. A slapping sound. *Whap whap whap,*
whap whap. A warm barley-scented wind, diesels idling,
an urgency akin to salmon rushing up a torrent,
toilets flushing, *whap whap whap*, against the nightstand.
I open my eyes, and inches from my face the smiling jowls,
the leaping salmon of Lulu's tongue grazes my cheek.

Big trucks are pulling out of the parking lot
as Lulu looks for just the right spot. A few miles north
screens are lighting up and the search begins again
among the roots and branches of family trees

where the whirr of spirits jostling for places among the saints
might sound like a great flock of winter starlings.

Here beside the highway the living trees release
real birds into the morning air. After a bowl of kibble
and two bowls of water for my ever-ready friend,
we join the snowbirds migrating south. *Snowbird,*
a mildly pejorative term for the retired, the still mobile
aged who flock toward milder climates at the onset of winter,
whose hair may be white or whitening. Also slang
for someone addicted to cocaine or heroin.
Having resisted the latter, I am becoming the former.
My wings this morning are the fenders
of a late-model Honda belonging to my friend Bill,
who is already enjoying the sun of Santa Barbara, plucking
one true sentence, and then another, out of the air,
puffing a smokeless electronic cigarette and sipping
perhaps a cool glass of sauvignon blanc,
while the relentless tides gnaw away at the sandy bluffs.

A long time I have loved the desert, great swaths
of open lands once ocean, now with waves of sculpted sand
and stone brushed and coifed with color in the mid-morning sun,
smoky blue drifts of sage fading into pale green creosote barrens
where a deep quiet resides.

Like a fleck of silver glinting in the sun, we stream down
the interstate. Out the windshield, the Sevier Desert,
the Cricket, Mineral, and Wah Wah Mountains to the west,
the Pavant to the east, rising and falling waves stilled
into plateaus and cliffs, canyons, pillars, hoodoos, and arches
shaped over time by wind and water. I'd like to turn off
at Beaver and revisit those geological wonders,
but we're going to Santa Barbara. A glimpse
of the Pink Cliffs, a memory of Zion, a campfire and stars fading

to a dawn walk among the hoodoos at Bryce—I'll hold
the wheel lightly and climb the Escalante Staircase
to the cadences of Led Zeppelin.

Hummingbirds, I've heard, can fly across the Gulf
of Mexico on less than one-tenth of an ounce of fuel.
And a bear can sleep through the winter in a snowbank
without having to get up to pee. The spadefoot toad
can lie dormant in a dried mud hole in the desert
for as long as six years waiting for the rains. (Once
in cactus foothills west of Tucson I followed the sonic rainbow

of their bleating to a big puddle at the base of a saguaro
and observed their frenzied mating.) Certain spiderlings
can release threads of silk from their abdomens and balloon
on the wind for over 1,200 miles. But the car needs gas,
and after three hours of driving both dog and man bladders
tend also to balloon.

We pull in under the sign of the dinosaur,
where a phalanx of big rigs idle in the sun, Macs, Whites,
Fruehaufs, giant segmented varicolored vaguely malevolent
caterpillars dozing on a dirt lot. This pit stop in the desert
is as thrilling to Lulu as a night at the cinema. She pulls me
with her hunter-orange leash toward the dusty bushes.

This day is a movie that won't be made.
Even surrounded by the sunny balm and healing quiet
of the desert, this truck stop gives off such an authentic
sinister vibe Hollywood should know about it.
At the far end of the lot another road-disheveled lone traveler
walks his terrier. Brother, I think, as Lulu loads up,
I wouldn't stay here long. Follow us up the on-ramp
and down the laminate interstate past Paragonah and Parowan,
past Summit, Enoch and Cedar City, past Kanarraville,

New Harmony, Pintura, Toquersville, Leeds and Quail Creek,
and past St. George, where bulldozers work around the clock
leveling lots for snowbird nests, then down the steep descent
out of Utah to that isolate corner of Arizona
where the Virgin River cuts its canyon through red sandstone
and out into the Pacific Time Zone.

The speechless sun that lights the topmost feathers
of the raven and makes a light sheen on the miniscule
leaves of creosote greening the near and far undulations
of the land lulls the driver into a waking dream: late fifties,
two fathers and their sons cruising a two-lane
in the pre-dawn darkness of the San Joaquin valley
heading north to hunt pheasants. Hum of tires
on tarmac, low whirr of the heater fan, rocking motion
and road-sway, scents of kenneled dogs, black coffee,
my father's pipe, and the low talk of men.

We bump off the road onto a dirt track and rouse
from the torpor of the drive as the sun begins
to spread its fan above the Sierras. We unload the dogs,
load our guns, and survey the long rows of shoulder-high
corn stubble. Strange how beauty, tenderness, violence
and ignorance can be strands of the same rope braiding
or unraveling a day. Fatherless himself from the age of two
when his father, the big-league ballplayer died, he was
a teacher and coach, master of the slow curve
and the knuckleball. Having had his fill of guns
in the South Pacific, this was the only day
we ever hunted together, following the dogs
down the dusty corn rows. I carried an old double-barrel
12-gauge, and when the first pheasant burst
from the stubble I swung the big gun at the streaming
blur of feathers and yanked both triggers

so that the recoil from the double blast knocked
the gun butt into my skinny shoulder like the rear
hoof of an angry mule, lifting me in my boots
and slamming me down in the dust. I held on
to the gun, though it seemed much heavier.

The bruise on my shoulder, in the days that followed,
seemed to change color like a slow sunset under
the skin, a blue-green glow reddening and darkening
to black night on an island the rising waters
rose above and slowly swallowed. But it was
my father who suffered most that day. The pheasant
he knocked down at forty yards in the first light,
with a clean kill-shot, turned out to be a great horned owl.

Oasis. A word that opens its slow circle, exhales,
brightens like a ripening plum reflected in a pool welling up
from underground springs. Coptic in origin, translated from Egyptian
into Greek, soughing out of the desert, the land's breath
graven in books, blown by breezes and whirlwinds,
carried around the globe in the shimmering mirages
of dreaming minds, erected on steel poles, paired with green
iconic palms and outlined in neon above the American desert.

Oasis Hotel and Casino, Mesquite, Nevada, sits by the interstate,
a cement and stucco sarcophagus, haunted by dead kings, queens,
and jacks of bad bets. The Oasis gone bust, a For Lease sign
outside. Inside pairs of ghostly pineapples, cherries, crowns
waiting for their prodigal triplet to line up again in the slots
and spew coins, a small transitory joy announced by flashing lights
and sirens. This desert is full of ironies, small and colossal.
Vast waterworks of Las Vegas, replicas of the fountains of Rome,
the canals of Venice, pyramids of Egypt, a volcano that erupts
every seven minutes, Siberian tigers pacing behind glass

interior walls of a hotel foyer. "Vexilla Regis prodeunt inferni,"
(banners of the King of Hell draw closer) Virgil tells Dante,
"therefore keep your eyes ahead." In the rearview mirror
I see Lulu calm as a tortoise basking in the sun on Yucca Mountain,
the Oasis fading, waiting for the next big boom.

We pass through the Moapa River Indian Reservation,
north of the Muddy Mountains and the Valley of Fire State Park.
We drive in ignorance through the simplified histories
of the land and its actual people flashing by on roadside signs.
We're making good time. To the north the Desert National
Wildlife Range, the Sheep Range, butts up against the Nellis Air Force
Bombing and Gunnery Range. We slip into the thickening traffic
of Las Vegas.

Las Vegas awash in afternoon sunlight
seen in tunnel vision through sunglasses at sixty miles an hour,
more or less, from the shifting lanes of the interstate
is reduced to the mad graph of its skyline, steel
and glass facades, concrete plains and asphalt meadows,
plastic bags, styrofoam cups, and a pair of Nikes
hanging from a powerline. The pull is toward the Pacific,
up and out of Nevada over the mountain pass, four lanes
of traffic pushing the limit to see who can be first
across the state line. For Christ's sake, watch out
where you're going little red Corolla—we swerve
into the breakdown lane to give her room, give her the horn
instead of the finger, wave never mind never mind,
we're still alive driving into a slow California sunset.

Before long we're in Baker, desolate bastion of cheap motels
and pricey gas where the broken wagon wheel and the neon
palm tree sputter above vacancy signs. No thanks, we think
we'll push on to Barstow.

Before Lulu and I stopped for the night at the Holiday Inn
Express motel, before the interstate smoothed and sped the way,
before old Route 66 was an American icon and a song
by Bobby Troup, before the Southern Pacific and Atchison, Topeka
and Santa Fe railway, before the miners and gold seekers,
before the twenty-mule team borax wagons,
before Camp Sugarloaf, Grapevine, and Waterman Junction
was renamed for William Barstow Strong, the rail magnate,
Barstow was a seasonally green river bottom frequented
by the Mojave, Paiute, and Chemehuevi tribes. Chemehuevi,
a name that asks to be repeated, a name in the Mojave dialect
meaning "those who play with fish," and in Quechan meaning
"nose-in-the-air-like-a-roadrunner." They call themselves Nuwuwu,
"The People." Their language, like those of so many
Native American tribes, is nearly extinct. But the people live
their lives and Barstow thrives.

After a fine dinner of enchiladas, rice, and beans
at a Mexican diner on the Barstow business loop, Lulu
and I walk the vacant lot bordering the motel,
and the warm dark vastness of the desert night
whispers in Chemehuevi tongues. I feel the inquisitive
pull of the night, the tug of Lulu's leash toward the scents
of the river bottom, purslane, and mint and just a hint
of cedar smoke from a distant campfire. Beyond the pools
of halogen light, black Lulu is invisible now, pure energy
flowing like a rivulet, meandering among clumps of brush
and stunted salt cedar toward the river, the dark Mojave
lit only by the faint light of stars. I think if I let her she'd
walk me all the way to the Pacific, to the cliffs at Santa Barbara.

Strange things can happen in the desert at night.
One can suddenly begin to understand a new language,
can begin to hear and comprehend in the murmuring

of distant water or the rustle of brush stirred by a faint
exhalation as vague as a pulse from the stars, a voice,
a rhythm and a tone, as though one's own footsteps
released from the dust and gravel some long dormant
soliloquy or some prescient recitation from a time to come.
It is as though the black dog night pulls one deeper
into the night until the night is no longer dark
but luminous with metamorphosis and one steps
out of the body and ranges freely as pollen in the wind.

Day three. Dream and memory swirl like a dust devil
in the pre-dawn flow. A boy of eight, I open the motel door
and step quietly out into the dirt parking lot in Lovelock, Nevada,
where a heart-shaped sign, buzzing like cicadas, is pierced
by a red neon arrow. A flock of wild turkeys,
bowed, bobbing, and mumbling like monks at prayer,
amble across a square of bright green grass toward the desert.
I hunch over and stealthily pass between our Buick and a Ford
and join them, imitating their rhythmic bobbing movement,
my eyes half closed, shoulders hunched, feathers still
and swept back along my arms.

Whap whap whap against the bedside stand—Lulu's tail
sounding its eager alarm. I open my eyes to her black muzzle
panting Santa Barbara Santa Barbara. Maybe by now
she can smell the ocean in the lightest breeze wafting in
from the west. Just past 5 a.m. If all goes well, by noon
we could be standing at the edge of the continent hearing the rush
of surf, watching the blue waves curl against the rocks.

After a light breakfast beneath the smoldering fires
of the Middle East in the motel lounge I load the Honda,
leash Lulu, and we walk out to the edge of the desert.
In the pre-dawn light the silhouette of a man and dog
dissolve in the distance.

A smooth road inspires reverie. Old songs on the radio
work like a siphon on the roadside ditch of memory.
A rare summer rain on the Mojave forty years ago
shut down work for the road crew based in California City.
Three young workmen, with an unexpected day off, bored,
exhilarated by the rain, turn prankster. They drive out
into the desert east of Edwards Air Force Base with a six-pack of tall boys.
They swerve among glistening carapaces as the rain floods
the burrows of desert tortoises, and a bad idea strikes
like a gong: let's load them up in the truck and release them
on the main drag of California City. It'll be like the biblical rain
of frogs. They'll take it as a sign of the end times,
a tortoise hoard like a slow parade of the damned.
Damned stupid idea like so many others. Go back to the motel, boys.
Watch some baseball. Rest up. This break won't last.

Lulu, here's something from a long-gone childhood
you might appreciate. Stanley Woodman, stepfather for a time,
jack of all trades, pilot, home builder, con man, entrepreneur,
Lancelot of many start-ups: Stan's Sonoran Adobe Bricks,
Stan's Sand and Gravel, Stan's South Bay Salvage, Stan's
Small Airplane Repair, Stan's Gulf Guide Service, Woodman's
Pauma Valley Contracting. He was a big sandy-haired
ex-football player, sweet with children, rough on women,
smooth dealer of all sorts of deals gone wrong.
Not afraid of hard work or long hauls, Stanley Steamer
the Dreamer Mom called him. For years he kept us moving,
a step or two outside or ahead of the law.
For a time we lived in *La Casa Contenta*, an upscale restaurant
closed for the year. The owners were off on sabbatical in Europe.
We served as house-sitters, caretakers, living in high style
compared to the one-room flat with a Murphy bed and hotplate
above a cigar store and pool hall in Old Redondo Beach.
La Casa Contenta, an unlit neon sign on the valley road,

a gravel driveway lined with ponderosa pines, a sprawling
California ranch house with a river-stone fireplace,
a long dark mahogany bar and living room turned lounge
with a pair of nine-foot sofas and several overstuffed chairs
under slow-turning ceiling fans, and two big bathrooms
down the hall marked *Ladies* and *Gentlemen* in gold script.
My room was the coat room just off the entrance, my bed,
the padded waiting bench, a cigarette machine, 25¢ a pack,
with chrome pull-handles, one for each brand, Camel
to Viceroy. My best friend was a collie named Roddy.
He had a big shaggy mane like a lion. He slept on the floor
beside my bed in the coatroom, trotted alongside as I rode
my black fat-tire Schwinn through the valley.
Once we saw a group of boys dropping kittens from a roof.
"Stop that, you assholes," I yelled. They do stop, and look at me
surprised by the pint-sized intruder in the midst of their
modest experiment with gravity and cruelty. They clamber down
from the roof and charge toward me, but Roddy's fierce demeanor
and low growl stops them. A big dog is a fine companion
for an impulsive boy. Human cruelty takes many forms
and is often motivated by the best intentions. Forgive me, Lulu.
I rode off into the sunset muttering *sons of bitches*.
Somehow Stan got a heads-up that the Sheriff was coming
in the morning with a subpoena. Before dawn I was loaded
in the back of the Buick with the essential luggage,
and from the rear window watched Roddy,
tied to the front doorknob, watching me as we drove away
from *La Casa Contenta* for the last time. I must have cried
all the way to Kansas. When it comes to loyalty, dogs outdo us.

We get off the interstate at Victorville and somehow
take a wrong turn. Apple Valley? That's not right.
We pull over and study the map. Soon we're on the two-lane
Pearblossom Highway rolling up and down over the desert

through stands of Joshua trees. All along that highway
you can see the dreams gone bust. *For Sale* signs
fading in the sun, staked foreclosure notices on the gravel driveways
of unfinished ranch houses on 2½-acre lots. Whole neighborhoods
of modest abandoned homes on streets named Buena Vista
and Agua Prieta, with here and there some holdout family
in a double-wide with two or three junkers in the yard.
Say sunshine is money, and they're all millionaires.

Past the last *For Sale* sign, Joshua trees' morning shadows
stretch out inviting us to pull over and walk among them.
I open the car door and Lulu jumps out, instantly enthralled
by new ground and the complex scents of the desert,
tracks of sidewinders, kangaroo mice, and coyotes.
I unhook her leash and let her run. She leads me
weaving among creosote bushes and Joshua trees
to high ground where the railroad tracks shine. Raven black,
Lulu sits between the rails posing for a portrait of the morning.

An out-of-date road atlas conspires with poor signage
to lead the travelers astray again, and Lulu senses
that her friend has lost his way. We stop for gas
at a crossroads near Palmdale where a crowd of Latin
American workers wait for jobs. A white van pulls up
and a dozen men gather at the driver's window.
Among nodding heads and gesticulating hands, Spanish
cadences, "Si, Yo soy un trabajero bueno." The van door
slides open and three men climb in. The van drives off,
and nine men shuffle back to the shade of a Chinaberry tree
to continue their vigil.

It's hard to say much about the road not taken
except that it makes all the difference. Here's my theory
of road trip wrong turns: as soon as it begins to feel

wrong, stop, turn around, try to get it right. Don't keep
driving north when you want to go west. Sure,
there are detours, and wrong turns can lead to adventures,
new discoveries, as well as dead and dying ends.
But if it's Santa Barbara or bust trust your intuitions,
and if you are riding with a dog whose true companions
are within a hundred miles, pay close attention
to the dog's demeanor.

After two or three stoplights I look in the rearview
where Lulu's eyes say no, this is not the way to go,
then a sign, Edwards Air Force Base 26 miles. Not
the place Annick and Bill have gone to spend the winter.
Not NASA Bryden Flight Research Center. This is not
the space shuttle, this is Bill's Honda and Annick's dog.
As soon as I turn around Lulu smiles and settles down.
Highway 14, past Littlerock, Vincent, Acton, and Placerita
Canyon, out of the desert and into the coast range.
Then 118 through Simi Valley among the dodgers
and huggers, candy-apple Corvettes, Beamers, and black
Jaguars, back in the So-Cal car culture. Coastal oaks, palms
and eucalyptus, hibiscus, and ice plants along the highway,
and even I can smell the heart-wrenching salt breeze
off the ocean, and Lulu, Lulu knows, Lulu knows.

***

What is this joy at first seeing the blue-gray Pacific
shimmering toward the open horizon? There it is,
earth gone water, and the verge where the roads end,
two bodies skin to skin.

Four

TWO ENCOUNTERS

I. Buffalo Trace

Stars glitter across black pastures,
gleam and shine in the eyes of buffalo.
How many stars ride the dark dome
of a buffalo's eye? How many
buffalo breathe the scents of grass
and river mist, starlight glinting
in the frost on their dense curled coats,
on flecks of mica riding their hooves
as they move in clans and gather
along the trace that leads to the shoals
and shallows of the crossing? Is the river
of the Milky Way their map? What
calls them? Why, when they come
to the two canoes by the river,
do they jump over the first where a man
sleeps, and smash the second
with their hooves until it splinters
and bloodies the fore bones of their legs?
Why do they spare him?

II. Bird in the Hand

Cold still sunlit hour, December
in the Bitterroot. The sun was about
to let the Bitterroots rise up in front of it,
the moon was rising over Kentucky,
shining on the river where the Buffalo
used to cross, easing up the east slopes
of the Sapphires. Chickadees flew
back and forth from the apple tree
to the feeder, picking up sunflower seeds.

One flitted across my head twice,
thanking me, maybe, for filling the feeder.
Up in the bare branches the birds
picked open the seeds. One chickadee
was looking at me. I made my chickadee
sound, took a handful of seeds from the bucket
and held out my open palm flat and still.
The bird landed on my middle fingertips.
I felt the delicate cleaving of its small
clawed feet. It looked into my eyes
hopped into my palm and took a single seed
then flew back to a branch in the apple tree.
Ah, Chickadee, now that was something.

PORCUPINE DOZING

Little velcro-like seeds of hound's-tongue
in the soft gray underfur
and the black-based golden quills
lightly trembling like a clump
of stiff grass and the black eyelids closed
on the black eyes dozing
or playing dead in the grass
beside the refuge trail.

Young dark inside-out pin cushion,
be careful, the dogs are coming,
dragging people on leashes.
Things could get snappy.
Some dad might test his shoe leather
against the stilled bush of your wintry defenses.
Some dad's dachshund all day pent up
might come grinning, following his nose
right up your rear quills, then,
as to human kindness and animal cuteness,
all bets are off.

Why think now of the Siberian tigers
pacing a small space behind a glass wall
in the vast foyer of a Las Vegas casino?
Or the one with a coat of snow and shadow,
tracked, darted, and loaded in a crate,
its power conscripted to sell tires on television?
Your bundled body in quiet camouflage
needs the right background in which to disappear.

We should lift you with our minds
back into the pine tree and let you sleep.
We should bow to you at a distance
honoring the peculiar earth spirit

you are. We should pet you
with our hands in our pockets.

BREAKING THE LULL
Captiva Island, Florida

Flying out over the Gulf in the yellow
Piper Cub with pontoons, all speech

drowned out by the engine, my stepfather far away
at the controls, I gripped the vinyl seat

and looked out cautiously on the water, blue-green
and tracked by the breeze in ripples

stylized as engravings in old books.
Then the wings dipped suddenly to the right,

the Gulf lifted its scarred face
and looked me in the eye. You

won't live forever, it said, as the plane
rose again, nosing up into a stall

until the engine sputtered and popped
and went quiet long enough for doubt

to take me wholly in, before we dropped
down toward the blue-green wall

of the Gulf and the propeller caught
in the rush, the engine groaned,

the yellow wings held their tremulous grip
on the air, and we headed out toward Mexico

where my stepfather, proud pilot, strong-armed
and mostly kind, father of my younger brother,

disappeared a few years later. This time
tracing the boomerang shape of Sanibel Island

we made a slow turn back to Captiva
to buzz the house set in sea grapes, sabal palms,

and tall sweeping Australian pines, where my mother
lay resting in her bed. The sound of the plane

shrill above the trees, breaking the lull,
must have annoyed her, must have caused

our devout neighbor, Miriam Johnson,
to add a note of insistence to her afternoon

prayers, and her husband, Belton, to stop
mid-stroke, as he applied a third coat

of gray marine paint to the wooden hull
of his boat, and look up from under

the brim of his hat at the yellow
airplane loud against the blue,

its long pontoons nearly clipping the treetops,
its wind erasing the widening rings

of the parrot fish feeding in calm water
by the dock, disturbing the slight glow

around the pollen-laden pistil
of the hibiscus blossom, and the glint of sun

on the earrings of José Gaspar and Black Caesar
leaning on shadows in the mangroves,

and big bills tucked in breast feathers
of pelicans guarding serenity on all

the pilings at the end of the pier,
propeller and pontoon catching there

and tearing the fabric of that stillness
made of many stillnesses.

FLOOD

I'm with Keats watching
the moving waters at their priest-like task.
Still, it's hard to praise the waters when they rise
above all human significance, when the houses
are torn from foundations and drift off in the flood
with someone's mother and her cat clinging
to the shingles crying for help, the safe harbor
that was her home become a bad boat.

A child reared and rooted in the highlands
of Kentucky of a Baptist father born in Beaver
and a Baptist mother born just across the border
in Isham, Tennessee, my mother migrated
with her family, when the coal in McCreary County
petered out, to the coal camps carved in the hills
above Hazard. Her most vivid memory as a child
was standing on a hillside in the rain watching
a house plucked by the flood floating away
on the Kentucky River, a woman she had seen
before but didn't know calling from the roof.

My mother believed when trouble comes,
as trouble will, we should lean on hope
and stay alert, and when all is well it makes sense
to worry. She took that woman's hand in hers
and when the flood subsided and the coal camps
of Hazard went bust she held that hand
like an invisible friend on the train to Cincinnati.

If my mother were still here, I'd ask her
how long can one hold the hand of one who's gone?
How long between the drought and the flood?
Does the mule with muddy withers standing
on the shade side of the woodshed fear the sound

of passing trains? What was it like as a girl
leading your invisible mule through the streets of Cincinnati?

GURU

She was a sort of guru
of hula hoops instructing
the group of slightly younger

hula hoopers in the art
of whirling and twirling the hoops.
She could start the hoop

spinning around a wrist
then work it over her shoulder
slip her arm out

and spin it around her neck
then reach up through the hoop
and work it down her torso

to her hips her thighs her knees
her ankles then step out
with one leg and keep it spinning

with the other, kick it into
the air, catch it with her
other wrist and go all the way

around again with ease,
all the time smiling
and talking to her students.

SUNDAY AT THE SWIMMING HOLE

Leon wears a broad-brimmed straw hat
and nothing else. Among forty nude bathers
he seems overdressed, an intruder
with a movie camera panning slowly
the splash and ripple, the sun-glint of droplets
and streaming rivulets moving the light
along the contours of bodies, pert and pendulous
breasts and patches of pubic hair in many
clamorous human hues, everyone present
unclothed in bald joy this Sunday
at the swimming hole in the hills above Lagunitas.

A young mother with auburn dreadlocks,
creped belly skin not yet healed into stretch marks,
nurses her baby on a sun-warmed rock.
A hairy-chest buffalo of a man stands
nipple deep in the pool balancing a naked toddler
in each hand as though displaying trophies
for the camera. Leon zooms in to catch
the toddlers' contrasting expressions,
like the universal sign for the theater,
one a mask of tragedy, *daddy put me down,*
the other comedy, *daddy hold me higher.*

And the dog, Keats, in a wet red bandana,
leaps from a rock, twists his body above the water,
kicking out his four feet to adjust his flight,
snatches a yellow Frisbee out of the air.

A slim man with shoulder-length hair
finger-picks a riff on his battered guitar.
Notes drift through the air, blend with sun,
rise and fall and hover over the water.
A woman with a slight smile turns

from the camera and wrings water from her dark hair.
Leon's lens studies the grip and twist
of her fingers, one with a sapphire ring,
and the dripping jewels of water, the swirl
of her ear taking it all in. Amen.

RAIN, GOOD LUCK, MONEY, DEATH

Chirping like birds or electric bells
crickets in the high grass.
A slight breeze rustles
the cottonwood leaves, trembles the aspens.
Far-off sounds of a mower, a dog
barking, a flicker yodeling, but crickets
are the dominant composers, calling for mates,
asserting their charmed presence.

Now they stop as another presence
moves through the grass, crackling leaves
underfoot, and another chirping sounds—
a wild turkey, omnivorous, and the crickets
know to be silent.

Crickets are said to bring rain, good luck,
money, death. One of China's
boy emperors kept a cricket
for a pet in the folds of his gold robe.
Álvar Núñez Cabeza de Vaca wrote
in his journal that the sudden chirping
of a cricket on board his ship
heralded the presence of land
just as the stores of fresh water had run out.

The turkey ambles off
down the slope and the crickets
start up again, rubbing or vibrating
their wings against each other,
making their music with the little prongs
on their stridulatory organs, veins
that run along the bottom of each wing,
wings like acoustical sails
that trill and charm the morning air.

SUSTENANCE

First time I spoke with my neighbor Ted
on the road by the mailboxes I said, "Beautiful view
of the mountains." He said, "You can't eat the view."
For nearly thirty years I've found sustenance
in looking at those mountains. Those mountains
where a road follows a river through
an immense wilderness, forests, alpine meadows,
creeks, stands of giant firs and cedars.
Just a few yards off the road there are lush places,
hot springs, mineral licks where animals gather,
dense shady groves where time moves on
wild and secret paths just the way it has
since before there were clocks. So, what
are these trucks hauling up the road?
Three hundred tons of imported equipment
per load to strip bare, burn and debond
the chemical broth of earth, on their way
to the boreal plains of northern Alberta,
nesting grounds for millions of birds
bulldozed into toxic ponds and tar pits.
The Athabaskan watershed trashed and poisoned
like the southern marshes for the profit of …
You know where this is going, don't you Ted.
Let's invite the birds to the meetings.
Let's place glasses of Athabaskan river water
for each padded chair. Let's have the next
board meeting on site beside the sludge ponds
and project pictures of the land before the work
started. Let's explain again what runs on clean air
and water, and what runs on oil. Let's call
the elders and children of the local tribes
to report on our progress for seven generations.

For years I've argued with my neighbor.
It's time to invite him over for dinner.
Ted, I'll say, when he comes, make yourself
at home. I'll gesture toward the mountains,
raise a glass full of the color of sunset,
ching ching, bon appétit.

FANNY & ALBERT

For Fanny L. Kidney and Albert H. Pape

Miner with a flickering incandescent beam
On the hard hat of the skull, I go down and back
Into the mountain of moments to work a vein
Of glinting ore. While there is still time some spark
Of mica in the frontal lobes might open
To a place of light. Work this tool like a drill,
A hammer, into the wall that withholds. Or
Just sit awhile and listen. Listen until a voice
Comes clear, or music begins.

A magpie calls from the cottonwoods. No word
For the sound. A downy woodpecker clings
To the little wire cage that holds a suet cake
With seeds, a small impoundment where the link
Is clear between death and sustenance. I listen
To the quick pecking without looking. I don't
Want to make her nervous. She flies off anyway.
What a fine sound her wings make. I close my eyes
To the sun, feel the warmth, see a red glow
Through eyelids, like coals in a furnace. The link again.
To my left a northern flicker chortles. To my right another
Answers, then the sound of wings flying right
To left. I keep my eyes closed to the sun, drawing
In the warmth, soaking it up, floating in a red
Phosphorous glow, light through skin and blood.

A cold breeze plays on my cheeks and my hands,
And I am inside the great hemispheric dome
Of Union Station walking back in time, trying
To reach them. I am like one of the figures
In the bright mosaics, one moment posed in overalls
With a shovel and far-off hopeful gaze, the next
Walking among the crowds in the streets

Of the old Queen City of the West
Scanning the buildings on 9th Street for the Davenport
Club, where Albert intoned the words of Shakespeare
And Poe, and Fanny listened with her heart beating
To the rhythms of his voice. Later he would be
The one listening as she played a passionate
And flawless Mozart sonata, while the days
Of glory and gloom, nights of love and sorrow,
Hours filled with the sounds of trains that haul
The coal, the Chesapeake & Ohio, the cardinal's
Song, engines of time and timing, hammers
And drills of miners, builders, the swack and chatter
Of baseball waited, and my father waited,
And his father, and I waited to be born
Into the world they were making.

THE ROAD THROUGH THE MOUNTAINS

Tethered to alarm by the pagers on our belts, we waited for fire
to pay our wages. Somewhere up in the mountains lightning struck,
or someone's campfire offered a spark to dry wind.

We know what happened then. We packed our gear,
picked up those metal hats with wide brims, lined up
and boarded the green government buses,

looking tired, a little disheveled, nonchalant,
but no longer bored. We settled in for the long ride
into the Sierras.

The mountains veiled in bands of haze, the jokes and chatter
dissolving into the hum of the bus moving through miles
and miles of vineyards, orchards, pastures of the San Joaquin.

A few miles up a logging road our bus proved too long
to make a switch-back turn, hanging its right rear wheels
over a steep granite drop-off—another expedient official mandate

run aground for lack of foresight. Pickups and tankers ferried us
the last miles to the fire camp, where the chow lines were manned
by prisoners from Folsom or Soledad,

where we saw the flames crowning up the canyon
toward a stand of giant sequoias, two-thousand-year-old redwoods
we had to try to save from the blaze

with chainsaws, axes, Pulaskis, and shovels. The work we did,
the fire lines we cut, may have had some part in saving those last
big trees, like the ones you see the early loggers standing on

with their long crosscut saws, some grinning like conquerors,
but most just looking spent, like whalers lined up on the body
of the whale, providing a grim perspective.

Or, like that tree we drove through in our Pontiac station wagon.
See the boys in the snapshot? That's me and my brother Dean
climbing the still-living trunk of the giant sequoia before we knew
    anything
about work or worth, and that's the road we drove through the
    mountains,
the road they cut right through the trunk of that beautiful tree.

SPARROWS
Flamingo, Florida

Gray wash of waves against the seawall,
lap and splash of incoming tide,
whitecaps, blown wisps, salt spray—

a line of black-and-white skimmers
flying low, dipping down and cutting
the surface with the red scissors
of their bills.

This is as far as the road goes. Flamingo.
There's a boat launch and crabgrass
campground with tables, fire pits, palm trees
and birds everywhere. Gulls,
herons, snowy egrets, oyster catchers

and sparrows, the ubiquitous parking lot sparrows
of America. I was sinking
as I drove through the towns.

Now this warm wind in Flamingo,
this sparrow lightness.

A POOL OF MOUNTAIN WATER

If I were a still pool of mountain water
below a wall of rock with small fissures
from which a cluster of magenta bee balm
bloomed, the hummingbird who stopped in the air
just inches from my face, its wings ablur,
its iridescent green body shimmering
in sunlight, and looked into my eyes turning
its head slowly to get a good look
and saying a brief phrase or question
in hummingbird clearly to me, as if
I should understand and answer, I would
think it saw its reflection in the water
and marveled a moment at this other,
though I am no hummingbird or pool
of mountain water.

Or suppose I am all that I see, all
that I imagine, starting with a pool
of mountain water, a pool in a stream
cupped between boulders so the water
has slowed nearly to stillness and become
a dance floor for water striders, a mirror
for a bear, a hiker, or a hovering hummingbird.
Green moss on a rock, a bleached white bone.
When no one, critter or writer, is there
to define a reflection, the water still
holds the weather, the changing sky.
I loved being there when the hummingbird
came by. It seemed to have no fear
when it stopped in the air and looked
me intelligently in the eye. As for bears,
it's best to observe them from a distance.

ROOSTER SONG

Threads, the rooster, calls vehemently
repeatedly to whom or what, the sun?
Clearly, he means what he cries

through his tight cords and open beak,
his red pelt of throat and chest feathers
rising and falling with the shrill wind

of his song—strains of Coltrane
splitting the sax's reed.
Often his is the first voice I hear

at dawn, a voice different than other
roosters' voices. Blind Bob, Big Red,
Little Big Red, Wavelength and Threads,

all different cries—cockadoodledoo won't do
to call up their songs. They play
different instruments. The young cockerel

sounds forlorn as he tries out his song.
His pipes not fully formed, he can't
hit the high notes that Threads, the old-world

chanticleer, belts out lustily to the first light.
Once from a bridge above the flooded
Santa Cruz River, I saw a rooster

perched on the bloated body of a drowned cow.
It was hard to tell in the muddy rush
if he crowed, and he crowed over and over,

out of fear or joy. But he went on crowing
until he was a speck of red rushing away
in the flood, until he was nothing

but a small flare of memory lighting up
in another rooster's dawn song.

GOLDEN EAGLE

I saw a golden eagle
on a branch of a dead cottonwood
a couple of hundred yards

up the path. That's as close as I could
get before he flew
soaring out over the marsh

and toward the river, the blue
of the sky making, for a moment, a bright
contrast with the ruddy gold

of its neck and shoulder feathers, a sight
to hold for a while and then let go.
Tomorrow is Easter

that old festival that begins with the glow
of the dawn goddess rising in the east
worshipped by pagans celebrating spring,

an earlier incarnation of Christ,
the resurrection, the greening of the grass.
Now the birdlike cheep of prairie dogs,

Columbia ground squirrels, sentries at their task
of warning the rest of intruders,
walker in the path, soarer in the sky.

Even the great blue heron is a hunter
who preys on their babies.
Bad news from Patagonia, Jim Harrison died.

That golden eagle soaring away, maybe
that was Jim. He loved birds
and the idea of the resurrection

and kept his eye out for the smallest gods.
Bird and word brother, mentor, I'll miss you.
Jim the eagle soared out of the picture

over the river over the mountains over the blue
waves swelling beneath the bridge
he was building over the too-wide sea.

ORIGIN STORY

A light snow falls
      on layers of harder snow. Red,
a faint red of future fire,
      of beetle-killed pines, shows
through the bare cottonwoods
      where deer browse dried leaves
and branches and plunge their muzzles
      into the snow. One pregnant doe
beds down, and soon she wears
      a shawl of snow. Her ears survey
the distance. Then four others
      whose movements are so precise,
each step, each fluid turning of neck
      and shoulder, each scrape of hoof
through crusted snow, dissolve
      like clouds of breath into the woods
as light snow falls.
      Deep beneath them molten waves
of earth, and deeper still
      the teeming stars.

ACKNOWLEDGMENTS

Thanks to the editors of the following publications in which these poems first appeared:

Great River Review:
"Blood & Perfection"

Lake Effect:
"The Horseshoe Pier"

Mid-American Review:
"On the Job"

Miramar:
"A Field of First Things"
"Las Lomas"
"Road Trip with Lulu"

River Styx:
"Ode to the Letter R"
"When the World Began to End"

Sugar House Review:
"Mariposas"
"Peaches"
"Waking to Rain"
"Dandelions"

Talking River Review:
"Sustenance"
"The Road through the Mountains"

The Louisville Review:
"The Wreck of the Dominator"
"Not Like a Dream of Freedom"
"The Fence"
"Stars: Fort Apache / Theodore Roosevelt Indian Boarding School"
"Breaking the Lull"

Willow Springs:
"Aunt Godiva"

The following poems first appeared in the chapbook *Animal Time*, Accents Publishing: "Two Encounters," "Porcupine Dozing," "Sparrows," "A Pool of Mountain Water," and "Rooster Song."

ABOUT THE AUTHOR

Greg Pape is the author of *Four Swans, Animal Time, American Flamingo* (Crab Orchard Open Competition Award), *Sunflower Facing the Sun* (Edwin Ford Piper Prize, now called the Iowa Prize), *Storm Pattern, Black Branches, Border Crossings* (Pitt Poetry Series), and other books. His work has received the Discovery / The Nation Award, two National Endowment for the Arts Individual Fellowships, the Richard Hugo Memorial Poetry Award, the Pushcart Prize, and other awards. His poems have appeared in *The Atlantic, Colorado Review, Cutbank, Field, The Florida Review, Iowa Review, Literary Accents, The Louisville Review, Miramar, The New Yorker, Poetry, Kyoto Journal,* and others. He is Professor Emeritus at the University of Montana and former Montana Poet Laureate. He currently serves on the faculty in Spalding University's Naslund-Mann School of Writing. He has an MFA degree from the University of Arizona and an M.A. from California State University, Fresno. Born in California, Greg Pape has lived and worked in many places around the country. He has taught literature and writing at Hollins University, The University of Missouri, The University of Alabama, where he served as The Coal Royalty Chair in poetry, The University of Louisville, where he served as Bingham Poet-in-Residence, Northern Arizona University, Florida International University, and other colleges and universities. He has been awarded fellowships at The Fine Arts Work Center in Provincetown, the Centrum Foundation at Fort Worden State Park in Washington, and Breadloaf, where he was a Robert Frost Fellow. He has read his work at venues across the country and in Canada, Mexico, Italy, and Japan. His poetry reflects a deep appreciation for diverse landscapes and people, a love of animals, and an attentiveness to the natural world, which of course includes the man-made world. He divides his time between Frankfort, Kentucky and the Bitterroot Valley in Montana. He is currently at work on a new book of poems and a memoir.

OTHER BOOKS BY GREG PAPE

Little America

Border Crossings

Black Branches

The Morning Horse

Storm Pattern

Sunflower Facing the Sun

Small Pleasures

American Flamingo

Animal Time

Four Swans

www.ingramcontent.com/pod-product-compliance
Lightning Source LLC
Chambersburg PA
CBHW021652120626
46545CB00002B/826